Surendranath (Suri to all) was born in a village near Mudubidari in South Kanara District in Karnataka. He grew up in Davangere in Karnataka and had his education there. A graduate of the National School of Drama, he is a prolific playwright and director and a well-known name in Kannada theatre for over three decades. He has adapted many classics of world theatre from Ibsen to Shakespeare, Brecht, Frisch, Chekov, setting them in contemporary Karnataka to great success. He has published three short story collections, two novels and eight plays in Kannada. For more than a decade he was the programming head of ETV Kannada, one of the most popular television channels in India. For eight years, he was also the artistic director of Ranga Shankara, one of the leading theatre institutions and spaces in India. He is the recipient of the Ibsen Scholarship-2019.

Slices of the Moon Swept by the Wind

A novella

Surendranath S.

Translated from the Kannada by
Prathibha Nandakumar

Illustrations by Apara

SPEAKING
TIGER

TIGERBACKS | Speaking Tiger Short Fiction

SPEAKING TIGER BOOKS LLP
125A, Ground Floor, Shahpur Jat, near Asiad Village,
New Delhi 110049

First published in Kannada by Ankita Pustaka 2015
First published in English by Speaking Tiger 2022

ISBN: 978-93-5447-292-3
eISBN: 978-93-5447-293-0

10 9 8 7 6 5 4 3 2 1

Typeset in Garamond Premier Pro by SÜRYA, New Delhi
Printed at Chaman Enterprises, New Delhi

'The tears of the world are a constant quantity. For each one who begins to weep somewhere else another stops. The same is true of the laugh.'

—Samuel Beckett,
Waiting for Godot

INTRODUCTION: MY WORD

I admit it.

I had an aunt, my father's younger sister. She was a little short. All that I can remember of her now is her head with a mix of white and black hair, more white than black. The last time I saw her, she looked too worn out. Aged. Very aged. She was like the elder of the family, participating in every event at home. She was fond of talking, chatting. She was very fond of me. Whenever I went to her house, she would prepare some snacks for me. She loved to make my favourite—salted poha. Even in a financial crisis, she never failed to prepare this and served it with a great amount of love. She was fun to talk to. Her talk would be spiced with dollops of proverbs. She would not hesitate to say even some 'vulgar' proverbs in front of us boys. Of course, we could not understand them, then, anyway. We understood such words when we were in high school.

When I was a student at National School of Drama, Delhi, I used to come to Davangere once in six months and I could not return without meeting her. I could say I lost contact with her only after I stopped coming to Davangere. I had never seen her sharing her grief with anyone. I have only seen her smiling, never crying, never complaining. She lived her life without any complaint, grasping just a fistful of happiness. I really don't know how she managed to keep her family afloat amidst all the million problems. She was really a rare soul. Her family faced hardships one after the other, continuously. The family consumed a fistful of catastrophe along with their meals every day. This novel is loosely based on her and her family. I did not have the courage until now to write about her. She passed away some years ago and now I have dared to write.

I admit it.

Raghavendra Khasaneesa's Kannada short story 'Tabbaligalu' (Orphans) has haunted me deeply. I craved to write like that. I am not sure if this novel is a result of that torment. I went through agony after reading 'Tabbaligalu'. It is about a family that has come to Mantralaya to fulfil a vow. All the characters are defined by their relations—father, mother, younger brother, younger sister. Though they belong to the same family, they are strangers to each other. Every character is neck-deep in his or her own kind of absurd tragedy. The irony is that the family is united in the tragedy of the younger sister. No one believes in God. They go through the ritual of fulfilling the vow automatically; not with the belief that it will bring in something good, but with an attitude of a duty that has to be accomplished.

What disturbed me the most was the uncanny resemblance of my aunt's family with the family in the story. I felt like I had encountered the characters in the story, face to face. The characteristics and the structure of my novel are different, but the family in my novel may seem like it is straight out of Khasanees's story. Or a family that is familiar to me has come alive in his story. Both are dysfunctional families. They are families that are forever ready to face tragedies that could befall them any moment. I grew up in this kind of typical middle class, classical traditionalist Brahmin family. This type of Brahmin family is forever struggling to break away from the shackles of tradition, but always with one foot stuck firmly in tradition. These are families that are castaway, live eternally facing tragedies. My aunt's family had great belief in God and karma. They earned just enough to feed themselves. Happiness was measured by the fistful and anything beyond that was of no consequence to them. They lived for today, as if tomorrow never existed for them. Even when suffering from a deadly disease like herpes, they would endure the pain with total trust in God but never share their pain and sufferings with others. I have taken up the difficult task of writing a novel about such a family that went through a series of tragedies at every step. Had I not read Khasanees's story, it probably would not have been possible for me to write this. I am grateful to Khasanees's stories that portrayed characters that I had come across in my life, but gave a different vision to them. The few hours that I spent with him are the most treasured moments of my life.

Davangere is my place. The town that raised me and gave me my identity. My language is the language of Davangere. It is also the language of the world of my stories and their characters. Hence Davangere is the place where incidents happen in all my stories and novels. Those who are familiar with Davangere can identify and relish the details. However, if the reader is not familiar with Davangere, it does not make much difference also.

I am not sure what to call this, a novel, novella or long-short story? For now, I have decided to call it a novel.

Friend, journalist, poet and author Prathibha Nandakumar has translated this into English, managing to retain the Kannada-ness of the original. My thanks to her. I am grateful to Renuka Chatterjee of Speaking Tiger for taking this into the English-speaking world. Thanks to dear designer friend Apara for the drawings and to Prakash Kambattalli and Prabha of Ankita Pustaka, my Kannada publisher. I am indebted to all my friends who have been with me in my literary journey.

SURENDRANATH
Bengaluru, February 2022

They say nobody can understand what I say. I don't know how to talk straight. I keep talking a lot. As I keep talking, weird things happen in my head. Then I just drop it and start talking about something else. So, my teacher told me that I must write whatever I think of in a book. As and when I remember. That is why I am writing this. Sometimes I don't remember anything. I don't even know what day or date things happen. I write as and when whatever comes to me...

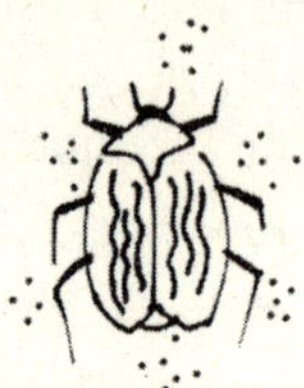

Appa, Amma, Doddakka (my first elder sister), Sannakka (my second elder sister), Tangi (my baby sister), Anna (my elder brother) and I live in this house. Doddakka is unmarried. She looks older than my mother. Actually, she looks very old. I believe I had another elder sister, but not anymore. If I ask why she died, Appa gets angry. Why do you need to bother about those things, he says. Appa rarely scolds me. In fact, he does not scold me at all. Only when I mention that other elder sister, he scolds me. And if Amma starts crying, she will go on till the next day. So, nobody can talk about the dead sister in the house.

Our house is very small. One room for Appa and Amma and one room for us children. I sleep in our room, with Doddakka and Sannakka. Tangi still sleeps with Appa and Amma in their room. There is a hall adjoining both rooms. Anna sleeps there. At one end of the hall is the kitchen. I have never seen it lit with sunlight. There is a small vent somewhere up above there that is supposed to be a window. No light comes from there. Sometimes, during the day, a squirrel falls in from there. At night, a rat. Even during the day, Amma or Doddakka light a lamp in the kitchen and cook. If the lamp is put off, it is pitch dark there. All kinds of noises are heard from the kitchen during the night. Must be a rat or a bandicoot, just go to sleep, says Amma. Sometimes when Appa gets very angry with someone, he makes that person stand in the kitchen for half an hour. Anna has stood there most number of times. He is adamant and does not give up, no matter what. I am very scared of the kitchen at night, scared enough to pee in my pants. The toilet is way over there in the backyard. I am too scared to go there alone at night. Appa, Amma, Doddakka or mostly Sannakka have to accompany me. Sometimes nobody comes. On many occasions, both Tangi and I have wet the bed. Our beds constantly smell bad.

We have a curtain on the door to the hall. It has three roses on all four corners. In the centre of the curtain is a big green tree, under which are five cows and leaning against one cow is a flute-playing Krishna. Amma had embroidered it long ago, I am told. The curtain is now somewhat frayed and tattered. Along with this curtain, there is a curtain made of glass pipes which shakes every time the wind passes, making a tinkling sound the entire night, as if the wind is dancing wearing bells. When the wind blows strong it makes so much noise that sometimes Amma ties it with a thread. Sannakka unties it in the morning. She does not like it to be tied. She stubbornly insists Amma should not tie it. Sometimes Amma and her have big fights about it. Fight means Amma scolds Sannakka and she, with a sulky face, does the opposite of whatever Amma tells her. Finally, Amma makes her sit with her and explains and then Sannakka becomes all right. Sannakka really likes the tinkling sound. When the wind blows and the glass tube curtain starts singing, she forgets whatever she is doing and stands in front of the curtain listening to the music.

Go past Setty's shop and the cycle shop, turn left and our house is the eighth or ninth from the far end. There is a playground at the other end of the street. You can enter the road only from one side. There is only one end of the road for both entry and exit. Amma says it is like Kourava's Chakravyuha. Our house has a four-foot compound wall. Only our house has a compound wall on this road. There is a guava tree adjacent to the wall. Its fruits, even raw ones, are very sweet. So, hordes of birds come to this tree. If I hold out rice in my hand from the single window of our room, birds sit on my palm and eat. They are not at all scared. When

Amma gets angry she says, see how arrogant they are! Sometimes when the birds become too noisy, Appa bursts crackers. As soon as the cracker bursts the birds go silent for a minute. Then one bird starts making noise and soon all join at a high pitch. Again, it becomes very noisy. Appa may burst a couple of more crackers but he soon gives up, cursing. The birds have a field day making noise until it gets dark. We can't even hear each other talk in our room.

I believe I am sick. Appa takes me to Shetty doctor's clinic a couple of times in a month. It's always night time when he takes me. Shetty doctor speaks to me for half an hour. He speaks very softly. Sometimes when he speaks to me, he asks Appa to step out. After talking to me, he calls Appa in again and talks to him for some time before sending us home. Sometimes Appa cries bitterly. On these occasions, Shetty doctor hugs him tight and consoles him. And then Appa does not let me walk back home. Even when I insist on walking, he does not give in. He carries me home. He gets tired but doesn't give up. He stops every few steps, catches his breath and continues carrying me. I don't know what I suffer from. But Appa, Amma and Doddakka know. Anna also knows. Our neighbour uncle also knows. Or I don't know if he knows or not.

Once a beetle came into our house. Its body was all black. Green, yellow and black colours with blue lines. It was shining like a mirror. At first it was flying outside the window. Then it came in. It searched for a place to sit, but it looked like it did not find a place to sit in our room. It searched for a long time and then flew away. Sannakka said it must be caught and kept in an empty matchbox. Her friend did the same, it seems. If you shut it in a matchbox, how will it breathe? So, a small opening must be made in the matchbox. And if it gets hungry? Once in two days fill up the box with leaves from the jaali tree.

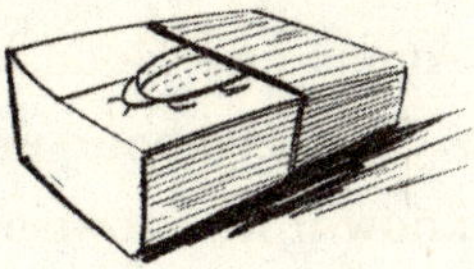

Appa also suffers another kind of sickness. At night, if there is any kind of noise by people or if anybody walks down the road talking, he wakes up from even the deepest sleep. He presses his ear to the door, listening. We are not supposed to make any noise at such times, not even whisper. If we make any noise, he will beat us. We are not even allowed to cry. Amma holds me and Tangi tight and sits in their room.

Mahatma Gandhi Circle is a little further up from Setty's grocery shop. Further ahead is Ashoka Talkies. We always take that route to go to Shetty doctor's clinic. I believe that after ten at night, lots of buses going out of town stop at Mahatma Gandhi Circle. Too much crowd and too much noise, I am told. Sometimes the noise is heard at our house also. I have not seen it. Come to think of it, I have not seen anything in this town. I have not gone out of my house at all. No, not that I have not stepped out, a couple of times I have gone out, but all those times are at night only. And of course, I have gone to Shetty doctor's clinic several times. I have not gone to school. Appa's friend comes home to teach me. On rare occasions, if I have to go out during the day, Appa covers my head with a towel and takes me.

From the window in our room, we cannot see the road. We can only see the neighbour's wall. Also the branches of the guava tree. From Appa's room we can see both the road and the guava tree. Appa has put a chair there, next to the window, specially for me. There is a thin curtain on the window. I slide the curtain slightly and keep looking at the road till I get bored. The curtain is so thin that you can see the people walking about on the road even without sliding it open. Appa has instructed me not to ever open the curtain completely. Mornings I have my bath, wear fresh clothes and sit on the chair. I get up for lunch. Then I sleep. Then the teacher comes. By the time the tuition is finished it will be evening. I don't go out. I sit at the window and watch the road. Sometimes I take rice from

Doddakka and feed the birds. Of late, even if I stand next to the window in our room, the birds come and perch on the window sill. I think they know me.

I love writing. I keep writing.
Tears in Amma's eyes in the kitchen
Every teardrop fallen on the floor
In front of the stove
Reflects Amma's eyes
All eyes open wide
And the kitchen is moonlit.

My teacher loves to read my writing. Appa says he does not understand what I write. Teacher loves me. He keeps telling Appa that I am very intelligent.

I am not like others. I know that. But I do eat like others. And sleep like them. I also cry. I play alone at home. Amma and Sannakka say I don't get angry at all. I look cute when I smile, says Amma. But I will not tell you how I look. It's for you to imagine any which way you want to. Whatever your imagination is, I look worse than that. I cannot see properly and need specs to read or write. Shetty doctor has got me special specs. If I just keep them on my nose, they stay put. I don't have an ear to use normal specs. In place of my ear there is just a hole. Seen from a distance, my ear looks like a mole.

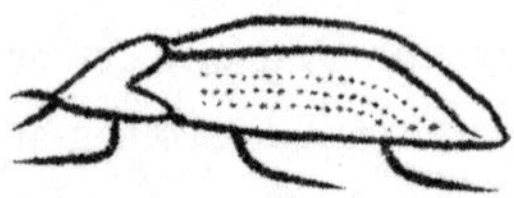

Anna is quite older than me. He does not talk to me much. When we are alone, he beats me, pinches me, calls me a pain. Once when he pinched me, Doddakka saw and I think she must have told Amma later. Next day Appa threw him out of the house. He was out the whole night. I don't know where he spent the night. But he was nowhere near the house. I believe Amma had searched for him. In the morning, he returned. He had his usual bath and went to school as if nothing had happened. He neither ate breakfast nor talked to anybody. That night, Amma made me sleep next to her. For a long time, she held my face in her hands and stared at me. Paapanna, how can you be silent without talking, clutching your teeth, okay, you don't tell us if someone beats you or pinches you, but how can you not cry at least? What could I say? I just smiled looking at her. You are one, you smile at everything, why did God punish you so? Honestly, I don't know what punishment God has given me. It is just that I am not like others.

Appa is not very talkative. He actually does not get angry at all. But when he does get angry, nobody can stop him. He will beat us with whatever he can lay his hands on. After that he sulks the entire day, feeling bad for hitting us. Sometimes after thrashing someone in the house, he goes away. Don't know where to, but he does not return the entire day. He returns late at night, after all of us have had dinner. After all of us fall asleep. Maybe he feels shame to look at us...

If something happens to Tangi, I will not spare God. I can't understand why He troubles us like this. If I get angry, that's it. Let Him do anything but not bother Tangi. Sometimes Appa says, it would be good if I believed in God, I could trust Him with my problems and keep calm or maybe God would believe me and do good to me. Sannakka offers a Namaskara from far away to God and that's that. Doddakka sits in front of God worshipping and meditating for not less than half an hour. In any case, each one in our house is either angry with God or talks to God or fights with or curses God.

Sannakka says she will not get married. She says that often. Sometimes she collapses and faints. This happens about twice a month. Poor thing. I believe it used to occur every other day earlier. It has reduced now, but not stopped completely. I believe it started when she was barely six months old. These days she just sits listlessly. Keeps to her work. Whatever Appa and Amma say, she does it. She is not bothered about others. She completes whatever task is given to her and comes into our room, sits leaning against the wall. She doesn't go into a deep sleep. She wakes up immediately anytime she is called. Come to think of it, I have never seen Sannakka sleeping properly. She wakes up abruptly even in the middle of the night. But in her work, she is very neat and tidy. When Sannakka cleans the vessels, you can see your face reflected in them. That shiny they become. A couple of times some people came to see her. After seeing the unmarried Doddakka they went away. Really, I don't know why God has punished Appa and Amma like this.

Sometimes, after my tuition class, Appa and the teacher sit and talk. I know very well what they talk about. Should I be admitted to school or not, if yes, to which school? Once Appa said, if I wish, I can be admitted to the school where my teacher is working. It is not that I am not interested in going to school, or in studying. Appa knows this, Amma too knows and even the teacher knows. Yet, at least once a month Appa and the teacher talk about school.

Appa does not like God and all that. He gets very angry when He is mentioned. If asked why, he replies, what pleasure has He given me in life, am I not enjoying all that he has given to my heart's content? But when Amma does pooja and all he keeps silent. Maybe he wishes at least Amma's worship could result in Doddakka getting married? All will be well once Doddakka gets married. Poor Sannakka, she is also aware of it. Amma says Appa was not like this earlier and even she does not know when Appa became like this.

One day the teacher asked me to multiply 18 eight times. 164. 22 multiplied by eight? 176. 64 multiplied by six? 384. 94 multiplied by sixteen? 1504. For a couple of minutes, the teacher went silent, then asked, do you know all the multiplication tables? Yes, I know. When did you learn? I don't know, I just got it. You have not seen the multiplication tables even once? I had seen it once. Then he sent me out. We used to study in the room I shared with Dodakka and Sanakka. I went into Amma and Appa's room and sat looking out of the window. When Appa came home, they closed the door and talked for a long time. I did not go out to see them. I was sitting in the room and was watching the street. Then Appa came into the room and sat next to me. He held my hand and sat for a long time. I kept looking at him and at the street alternatively. Four men were walking in the street talking loudly. They would halt every other step, talk and then start walking again. Only one man was wearing pants. The rest were in panches (a lower garment like a dhoti or lungi). One man had hung an umbrella on the back of his collar. Two of them were wearing leather chappals. One man, the one in pants, was wearing shoes. One man was wearing Hawai chappals. The last one did not speak for as long as I was watching. He was just nodding at the others' talk. Only he had crossed his hands behind his back. All of a sudden Appa started crying and hugging me. I don't know why, but I also felt like crying. But I was afraid to cry. I didn't cry. I thought looking at Appa would make me cry, so I looked out of the window. Now one stray cow was standing there. It had nothing in its mouth, but was chewing continuously. Its mouth was frothing a lot. After some time Appa calmed down and said, why are you born in our house, child, what sin did you commit to be born in this house? I smiled. The teacher said you are very intelligent, don't you like to go to school? I got scared, for some reason. I looked at Appa. I shook my head saying no. Appa did not persist. Never mind, if you do not want to go why should we pressurise you? Appa wiped his tears and walked out.

I am not good-looking. Everybody gets scared when they look at me. Even Tangi is scared to look at me. She does not come to me at all. I so much love to carry her but as soon as she sees me, she screams. So I never stand near her. Only when she is asleep, I stand beside her and look at her. She looks very cute. Sometimes Amma says, don't stare for long. Then I leave the place. Amma comes running behind me. I didn't mean in that sense, child, she hugs me and cries. That day Amma will cry the entire day. She will not talk to anybody. I don't know how, but Appa comes to know of it. He makes both Amma and me sit in front of him and talks to us. I know why Amma says that. Tangi is the only cute one in this house. She is still one and half years old.

She smiles even in her sleep. When she smiles, she looks like a sugar-doll. Actually, I don't know what a sugar-doll looks like. I believe it is very sweet. Even Tangi is very sweet. Amma is scared that may be I will cast an evil eye.

I was not born all right, I am told. There is no answer to why I am born like this. Amma says I was born on a new-moon day. Appa does not have such blind beliefs. That's another matter. I believe that night there was a power shutdown and it was pitch dark, nothing was visible. I am still not sure if the story is mine or some demon's. Just that it was a bad day and I was born all wrong. Appa had gone out of station. Amma suffered a lot of pain. Then Shetty doctor admitted Amma to the hospital. I believe Doddakka and Sannakka were both with her at the hospital. Amma suffered in pain for almost two days and finally I was born. Ayah wrapped me in a cloth. Her face had gone pale, Doddakka told me. Even Doddakka had panicked after picking me up and immediately gave me to Amma. Even she was scared of me in the beginning. Later on, she got used to me, she tells me now. The doctor told Amma not to have any more children. But Tangi was born. Thank God that was the end. As soon as she saw me Amma screamed out loud, it seems. Then she clutched me and started crying saying, this is my child, my child. Then the entire hospital came to know and all started coming to see me.

Amma and Doddakka had a tough time hiding me from their sight. They would roll me in a thin cloth and hide me. Finally, Shetty doctor shouted at everybody and stopped them. After Appa returned, we came home. Appa had seen me at the hospital. He did not speak at all, it seems. He simply held me for five minutes. He was talking to Amma as if nothing had happened. Finally, he brought us all home. Shetty doctor visited me at home and took care of me. Even now he is the one who takes care of me.

Appa has a small textile shop. My grandfather started it, I am told. Then, when my uncle, Appa's younger brother, slipped and got caught under the wheels of a bus and died, my grandfather's business was transferred to Appa. Grandfather had five sons and three daughters. After my uncle passed away my father is the only surviving son now. Appa's elder sister is staying in some place, I don't know where. I have never seen her. Once upon a time the textile shop was making good money. Later on, as big textile shops were opened in the town, our trade was hit. Only known customers continue to buy from us. It's not too bad. Appa says, no problem for food and clothes for the family. But he cannot go too easy on the expenses. Actually, it is my expenses that are heavy on the family. Doddakka has studied till third standard. Sannakka till sixth standard. They were not smart in studies. And Appa did not force them to study. Anna is very intelligent. He is always reading something or the other. I believe he stands first in class. He does not like me. I don't know why. If I enter the room, he goes out. Even if somebody else is present, he walks out. When he comes into the room, if nobody else is there, he calls me a pest and tells me to get lost Earlier, Appa, Sannakka, Anna and I used to sit for dinner together. Amma and Doddakka used to serve. I don't know why, Anna stopped eating with us, or rather with me. After we finish eating, he will sit alone and eat. If I am not there, that is, if I have a fever and do not eat, then he sits with the others and eats. Actually, I do get a fever some six or seven times in a month. Everybody knows that Anna does this on purpose. Appa tried to talk to him a couple of times, after all he is your younger brother, why do you act like this? Anna does not respond. When he gets really irritated, he gets up and walks out. Finally, Appa stopped telling him. He keeps to himself with his studies, books and all. In fact, he hardly stays at home, always spending time outside with friends and at school. He comes home only to eat and sleep.

Appa, Amma, Doddakka, Sannakka take care of me very well. Whatever special snack is prepared at home, I am given first. I get whatever I ask for. Sometimes I feel they cuddle me too much. I feel shy. Doddakka catches me tight and kisses me on the cheeks like I am a baby. If I say let me go, she teases me like oho, big man, feels shy and kisses me more. Holds me tighter. I suffocate under her tight hug.

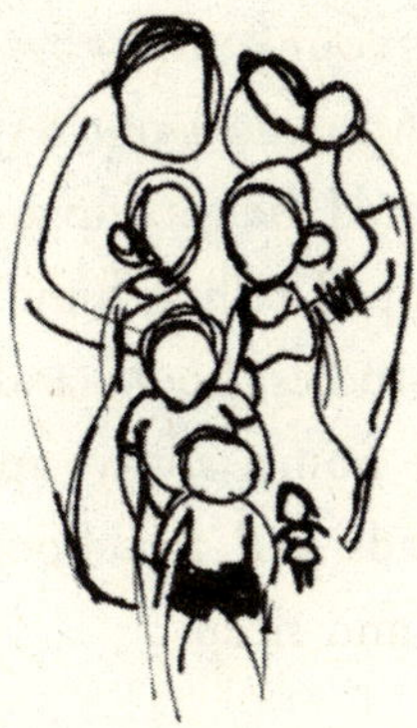

They say I brought good luck to our home. Appa's fortunes improved, I was told. The shop that was doing small business improved somewhat, Amma says. Appa does not believe in such talk. But Amma has faith. I don't know what improved. Looking at Sannakka, even I feel like crying sometimes.

Beetle is beautiful. I am not. Period.

It is not that I have never been to school. I had gone once. One day my teacher said I have nothing more to teach you, either you have to learn on your own or get admitted to a school. After that for a couple of days nothing happened. Then one day while having dinner, Appa told Amma, tomorrow give him a bath early and get him ready, I have to take him to school, I have spoken at the school. I didn't feel like eating dinner. It's not that I don't want to study. I also wish to go to school like others. But I know that people do not like me. I do not wish to walk in front of all the boys at school. Early next morning Amma woke me up and gave me an oil bath. My hair always stands out straight. My hair is like coir. It stays like that no matter how much you treat it with oil. Appa had said early but I learnt that day that early is 11.30 am. We left home at 11.30 and reached school a little before 12. Only after we reached the school, I understood why Appa had brought me at that time. There was nobody outside in the field. All were at class. Appa straightaway took me to the Headmaster's chamber. He made me sit in the anteroom outside and said child, sit here, I will be back in a minute. And went in. After a couple of minutes a peon came. He stared at me as he went in. I could see he was scared looking at me. After two minutes he returned, still looking scared. He gave me a side glance and went out. After he left a teacher came. Before entering the Headmaster's room, he looked at me. He did not scream. But his face paled. Within a second, he beamed a big smile and went in. Then Appa came and took me by the hand. Headmaster also glanced at me just for a second and shook his head. He looked at me just once. After that he looked only at Appa or the books in front of him. After two minutes Appa took my hand and walked me to the place where I was sitting before and went in again. For some four minutes I was sitting alone. Appa rushed out, picked me up and ran out. I knew that he was furious. He was talking to himself. Once we had come out of the school compound I said I would get down. Perhaps Appa was tired, he put me down. Appa was so furious that he forgot to cover my head with a cloth. I was walking next to him with my head bent. Appa continued to talk to himself, the boys will be scared to look at you he says, he does not want your intelligence, he wants only looks, I made a big mistake bringing you here, I will not send you anywhere, you study at home, after all you have my shop, no problem for food and clothing. He blabbered on. He dropped me at home and went away. He returned very late at night. I could make out he had cried a lot.

I have a thousand things to say
But I am unable to say
On my pillow there are
A thousand words
Maybe crying
All wet.

Everybody says we are all like this because Appa and Amma married within the family, that is, they were related by blood. My father is my grandfather's (my mother's father) sister's son. It seems, Appa's birth was an event. There was a thunderstorm on the day he born. It was far too cold. On the second day, Appa's body turned blue. Appa was born in the seventh month, I was told. Until Appa was ten or twelve, he was constantly sick. At the age of seven, he almost died. Even after surviving he suffered from one or the other ailment. Even now next to Amma, Appa looks puny. Appa's younger brother, the one who died under the bus, was also so-so. When bathing, he would scream if water fell on his head. Ajji, Appa's mother, had to wash his head. Once in a month or once in two months. When Ajji felt uncle was dirty she would give him a bath the next day. Appa had another elder brother, I believe. He hanged himself in the village. Very intelligent, they say. He was unmarried. Nobody knows why he hanged himself.

Once I had a dream. I take a basketful of dreams to the market to sell. Nobody buys a single dream. I return with my basket of dreams. On the way it rains. All my dreams get wet. They bleed colours all over my body. From that day all my dreams turned colourful. Once I spoke about it to my teacher. He said, it's not your dream, your thoughts are like that, you dream with your eyes open.

I have several names. Amma sometimes calls me Papanna and Papu. Appa calls me Koose (Little One). Doddakka calls me Baby. When she is hugging me, she calls me Rajkumara (Prince). Sannakka calls me Muddoo (Cutie). Anna calls me pain, sinner, wretched. Tangi is not talking yet. She only says Dadadadada. She flings her two little fists in the air and sings Gagagaga. I don't know what she will call me after she starts talking.

Examination time. Anna had left home in the evening, saying he was going to his friend's house to study. Usually, he would return early the next morning. This time he didn't. Knowing his behaviour, nobody worried about it. When he didn't return even after the lamps were lit in the evening, Amma got scared. No matter what fights or how angry he got, Anna would always return at night by dinner time. After dinner, he would once again go out for studies. Appa came home at night after shutting the shop and Amma told him. Appa went out in search of Anna. He returned very late at night. His face was grim. He did not speak. He drank a glass of water and sat in the hall. I sat on the bed in the room. Doddakka and Sannakka were standing at the door of the room. All of a sudden Appa said loudly, no examination, nothing. Then? Amma asked. He will not be coming to this house, he went to Madras, it seems. For some time, nobody spoke a word. Then I heard Amma crying bitterly. Now, don't sit crying, said Appa and left. Amma cried all night, sitting in the same spot. Doddakka and Sannakka sat in the room, leaning against the wall. Nobody at home slept that night. Appa did not eat. I think after that night, Appa gave up eating dinner. He just drinks a glass of water and goes to bed now.

I know very well how people react as soon as they see me. No matter how hard they try to hide it, they are either scared or disgusted. I can make out very well. Later, to hide that or pretend like nothing is wrong they put up an act and smile. I know that too.

One afternoon I was sitting by the window, watching the street. It was not yet lunch time. A man, maybe a lunatic, was turning round and round in the middle of the street. Sometimes he would scream, can't bear the burden of this penury. He went further down on the road. I could not see him properly. I had to bend. So, I bent down. Now I could see him. He was standing on the road, suddenly he lay down in the middle of the road, lifted both his legs, knotted them under his neck. I kept watching him, bent down. All of a sudden, my head reeled. I thought I was going to fall. I sat straight. My head continued to spin. There was pain. I thought it was because I was bending down and kept quiet. I felt like sleeping. I got down from the chair. I could not take a single step. I fell down. I don't know what happened after that.

There is a big photo of Sri Ramachandra Pattabhishekha. Rama is in the centre. Seethe is to his side. Lakshmana on the other side. Bharatha and Shatrughna behind Rama. Hanuman is at the feet of Rama. Once in a week Amma or Doddakka wipe it clean. A white and orange garland made of wire, the kind they make baskets with, adorns the photo. The garland has turned slightly black. The photo leans out of the wall a little. Once a pair of sparrows built a nest behind it. They were so noisy. They would fly out, fly back clutching something in their beaks and hide it behind the photo. Looked like a husband and wife. They would talk behind the photo. After a week they stopped coming. Their noise also stopped. Sannakka stood on a stool and checked behind the photo. The nest was still there. Sannakka and I waited one more day. The sparrows did not return. We were sure they would not return. Again, Sannakka stood on the stool and checked. She carefully brought out the nest. We found four white feather-like chicks, dead. That is why the sparrows had stopped coming. Even Sri Ramachandra had abandoned them. That day Appa said, He could not save the chicks behind his back and how will He save us? Sannakka took the nest out and threw it away. I don't remember any other sparrows building a nest behind the photo again.

I am not sure if I will get a separate moustache.
I was born with a beard and moustache.

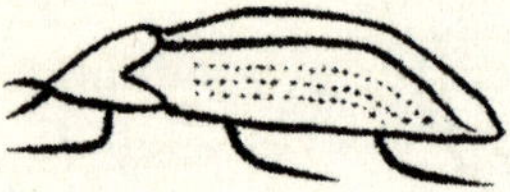

My baby sister dreams
And from her smiling lips
Slip out butterflies.

On the day of Muharram a procession passes through our street. It goes down the road to the end and returns the same way, passing by our house, twice. Some boys, as old as Anna, holding a rattle in one hand and a stick with colour paper stuck on it dance to a rhythm; sitting down and springing up and dancing forward. First comes a group of drum beaters. I watch it sitting at the window. I wait until the procession reaches the dead end and returns. That day also the procession came. The group was dancing. A man, slightly older than the other boys, was dancing very well. In between he looked in my direction. Even as he was dancing, he gave a smile. I moved a little away from the window and watched him. He moved on, dancing. I came out of the room and saw that the main door was closed. I realised he had seen me and smiled at me. I came to the window and sat waiting for the procession to return. After about five minutes the procession returned. Now, that man was not dancing but walking at the end of the procession. When he approached the window, he again looked at me. He smiled and waved his hand. I just kept looking at him. He had a scar, a black line, on his forehead. His eyes were green, not black like others. Until he moved away from the window he was looking in my direction. How did he know that I was sitting at the window and watching?

Day by day my headache is increasing. Sometimes it is unbearable. Amma lets me sleep on one lap and Tangi on the other. She keeps pressing my head till I fall asleep. Amma tells Appa, tomorrow take him to the doctor. Appa nods but doesn't say anything.

The sun is far too hot and bright. It is too hot no matter how one sleeps. Even with the doors open it is hot. Sannakka and Doddakka keep wiping their faces or fanning themselves with their saree edges. At least the hall is okay, sometimes the breeze passes by. For the past ten days I have fallen asleep in the afternoon in the hall. That day I was in a deep sleep and all of a sudden Amma screamed. I woke up. Amma threw the broom aside, caught me tight, pulling me aside. Hearing Amma's scream Sannakka who was grinding rice and Doddakka who was putting Tangi to sleep came running. Amma kept hugging me. A big scorpion was dead next to the wall. Amma had seen it while going from the kitchen to the room. The scorpion was walking towards my head. She had picked up a broom and killed it immediately. Why do such things happen to you, why is God against you, she cried. Poor thing, maybe the scorpion was feeling hot too and must have dropped down from the tiles above. If God wanted bad things to happen to me, it should have actually bit me, right? God sent Amma because he didn't want that to happen, right? So why should we blame God for everything?

Sannakka and I have a special place to hang out. In the backyard, next to the place where clothes are washed there is a Kaakada flower plant. I love to sit on the washing stone slab at night and look at the sky. It is very very quiet there. When I get sad, I go sit there. Sannakka also finishes her work and joins me. She has told me so many stories sitting there. Ekatrupa's story, the bear and the papad story, the kheer-setty story and all. Earlier Appa used to shout at us, why are you sitting in the dark? Now he doesn't. Sometimes when we get lost in talking and it gets very late and if we continue to talk even when he goes to the toilet, he says, go to bed. Sometimes we do not talk at all. Just sit and look at the stars in the sky. We count the stars. Sometimes I lie down on her lap and watch the sky. Sometimes she croons some bhajan in a low voice. Not loudly. Mostly she sings *Kangalidyatako* and *Sarasamukhi*. When I feel sleepy, she takes me inside.

I believe Appa was a great devotee earlier. He would not step out of the house without doing pooja. I don't know what happened, he suddenly got very angry with God.

Sannakka gets furious if anyone ridicules me. She cannot stand it. Once when I was sitting at the window, two boys who were walking on the road looked at me and laughed. One boy put out his hand towards me. He had peanuts in it. He called out to me, take, monkey, take, and started laughing. They started calling me names loudly. Sannakka must have heard it. She picked up a huge stone, quietly went to the gate, then screaming, she threw the stone at them. One boy got hit on his knee. Even I heard the noise of the stone hitting his knee. He fell down, then he got up and started running with a limp. The other boy had run away. Sannakka did not stop, she went a distance chasing him, caught him and beat him up badly. If people had not stopped her, I don't know what would have happened to him.

Whenever people came home with an alliance for Sannakka, Amma would casually send me to the room half an hour before their arrival. Until the guests left, I would sit at the window looking at the road. I don't feel bad at all for this. Let Sannakka get married, that is enough for me. Then of course Tangi. It is still a long way before they can talk of her marriage. Who knows what my fate will be by the time she gets married?

Once somebody came to 'see' Sannakka for an alliance. Like it always happened, Amma made me sit in the room and went out. For a very long time I sat at the window looking at the road. Somebody opened the gate. Somebody spoke loudly. And laughed loudly. Must be the guests. Amma was talking softly. Everybody must have gone in. I kept looking out of the window. All of a sudden, a boy's face appeared at the window. There was a woman with him. She had turned towards the road and was talking to someone. The boy held on to the bar of the window and peeped in. He saw me. For a second, we both stared at each other. Then he screamed out loud and ran away. The woman looked towards the window and must have seen me. She hurriedly went out of sight. I kept looking out of the window. Suddenly the door of the room opened with a bang and Sannakka barged in. She caught hold of my hand, dragged me out. They were all sitting in the hall. Including the boy and the woman who had seen me at the window. Sannakka held me in front of her and screamed, isn't he the one you saw, he is my younger brother, if you like, you marry me otherwise, get out. All of them walked out silently, without saying a word. Sannakka walked me back to the room. From that day she never allowed anybody to hide me in the room when we had visitors. But then, I never went out unless called.

Appa and Amma were talking. Doddakka was washing vessels in the backyard. Sannakka was cleaning the floor after dinner. I was lying down there. I was not yet sleepy. I had just closed my eyes and was lying down. Amma had Tangi on her lap. She usually grabs onto the tassel on Amma's saree, waves it over her face, sucks her thumb and goes to sleep. Appa and Amma were talking casually. All of a sudden Amma said, Papanna's headache is increasing, he must be shown to a doctor. Appa said I will take him to the Shetty doctor tomorrow. Amma caressed my cheek and started patting my head.

Doddakka's heels are cracked. Totally slit. Sometimes they bleed. She limps all over the house. When the pain gets intense, she sits down, leaning against the wall. Amma applies oil on her heels. You must see Sannakka's hands, they are like stones. Very rough. She says it never hurts. If you touch her palms it feels like sand. Tangi's hands are like warm milk. Amma's hands are also very rough. Once Doddakka's feet got so swollen, she could not walk. She had to apply some ointment given by Shetty doctor once every hour. Amma or Sannakka attended to it continuously. Once I sat down to apply the ointment. She said, why do you want to trouble yourself, rajakumara? Yet, I applied the ointment carefully. After applying the ointment, a bandage must be tied over it. After it was tied, she sat stretching her legs. After a couple of weeks, she was able to walk. The doctor said she should not wash clothes or vessels, and should not stand in water. From that day she stopped washing clothes and vessels. All that work had to be done by Sannakka. Doddakka now had to take care of cooking. Even that, she could do only sitting down. And cleaning the front yard in the morning.

For some reason Appa got entangled in a web of loans. He was always careful. There was some mistake in his accounts and he had to borrow money. None of us knew that he had taken out a loan. One day some people came home and created a ruckus and that's how we came to know. For a couple of days Appa did not even stir out of the house. He was that scared. After three days they came again. Appa made us say he was not at home. Sannakka told them. Looking at her, they didn't say anything. They had gone to the shop also and had made a scene there. Since they had not found Appa there, they had come home. Then they started coming home every day. Appa would leave home at 5.30 in the morning. Nobody could say when he would return. One day they came home and called out for Appa. I think there were three or four of them. I couldn't see properly from the window. Nobody had the courage to open the door. Anna was at home. All of a sudden, he came into the room. I was watching the road. Tangi was crying somewhere inside. The people were making a scene outside. Anna came into the room and called me softly, hey pain, come with me. I went to him. For the first time he put his hand on my shoulder and took me with him and opened the door. He told them Appa was not at home. The people stopped yelling and kept staring at me. I also stood staring at them. Their faces dropped. Anna said, he is my younger brother. They went silent and left. After two days they came again. Again, Anna did the same thing. Sannakka came to know of this. She shouted at him and created a scene. But Anna just brushed it aside and walked out. At night, when Appa returned home, she narrated the incident to him. He got so furious, I had never seen him that angry before. Anna was sitting as if he had not done anything wrong. Appa thrashed him with a ruler so bad that we could hear the bones cracking. Anna did not stir from the place where he was sitting. After thrashing him for some time Appa got tired and stopped. Anna got up and went out. He returned only the next night.

I was sitting alone on the washing slab. Sannakka could not sit with me. I looked up at the sky. It was filled with stars. Blinking. I stood up on the washing slab. They came nearer. I stretched my hands. There, I caught them! Had I been a little taller I could have touched even the sky. Like plucking guavas from the tree, I started plucking stars from the sky. I stuffed them in my pocket. I plucked so many stars that my shirt pocket felt very heavy. I got down from the slab carefully. I went in. As I walked the light spread. I went into the room. The room lit up. Doddakka was sitting, leaning against the wall. You look so beautiful, rajakumara, I have to erase the evil eyes cast on you, she said. There was a mirror on the wall. I could see my face reflected in that. I am not like me. I am very fair, with curly hair covering my head. I asked, who is that? Doddakka said, it is you, rajakumara. All of a sudden, the pocket gave way. All the stars had burnt out. They all fell to the ground. There was water near my feet. Very cold. The room was in darkness. I could not see myself. Scared, I screamed. Sannakka puts on the light. I am standing in the middle of the room. Doddakka is not there at all.

One day Anna came home, threw his book and sat down. Sannakka and I were playing Chowkabara. Doddakka was in the kitchen. Amma was putting Tangi to sleep and watching us play. Amma looked at the way Anna was sitting and asked, what happened? He said, Appa was sleeping on the municipal park bench, I had gone there with my friends at eleven to study, at two o'clock he got up and went somewhere, now I know where Appa goes to escape from the people he owes money to. Suddenly he got up and said, if he could not provide for us why were we given birth? Amma got angry. She said, why, are we not providing, bad times now, but he has not failed to provide food twice a day, don't talk nonsense, you behave like an enemy about Appa and Papanna. Anna muttered something and went away.

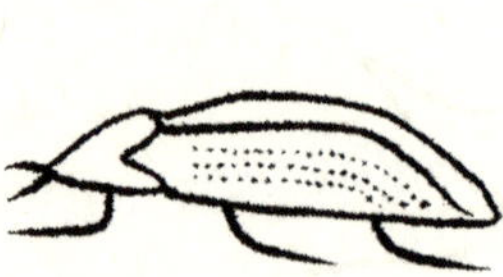

I wanted to drink water. Felt very thirsty. I went to the kitchen to drink water. Amma was sitting on the floor cutting vegetables. There was a bottlegourd. I looked at it. It was not round like other bottlegourds. It was long. In the centre it had collapsed like somebody had punched it. I felt it was just like my face. Instead of drinking water I stood and stared at it. Amma looked at me. I was standing staring at the bottlegourd. She asked why I was there. I didn't say anything. Crazy boy, she said, and she picked up the bottlegourd, broke it into two pieces and went to the backyard and threw it out. She returned and sat leaning against the wall, pressing her saree edge to her mouth and eyes and started crying. I sat next to her. I was silent. From that day on, I don't go to the kitchen when Amma is cooking.

For the past five or six days the people who lent money to Appa are coming more frequently. The other day a new man had come, not the ones who had been coming all these days. He screamed Appa's name at the top of his voice for the entire town to hear. He did not bang on the door like the others. Appa was not at home. Amma came running, scared, and opened the door. Sannakka followed her. Doddakka did not come out from inside. When I looked through the gap in the door, Amma was opening the front door. After seeing Amma the man started screaming louder, where is he, when he wanted a loan, he used to come four times a day, when I ask him to repay, he is missing for weeks, doesn't he know he has to repay the loan, I gave him a loan considering he is an old friend, but how can he be such a cutthroat? He went on and on shouting. I think Amma got scared hearing him shout. She went totally silent. Sannakka was standing behind Amma, holding on to her shoulders. Again, the man shouted, where is he? Amma really didn't know where Appa had gone. Appa never told anybody about his whereabouts. She just said, don't know, he went out early in the morning, but he will definitely return your money. Burn him, I say, will he really return it, he has been absconding, the man cursed. Then he must have looked at Amma's face, I could not see her face. Amma leaned on the door, if Sannakka had not held her she would have collapsed. The man went away without another word. That was the last time he came. Amma stood there holding the door. I knew the man had gone, so I came out slowly and looked at Amma's face. She was just staring blankly with her eyes wide open, without even blinking. Even when Sannakka pulled her she would not let go of the door. After some minutes she slowly sank to the ground, leaning against the door. Sannakka also sat down on her knees. I sat in front of her. Amma did not speak. The entire day she just sat there without speaking. At night when Appa returned she was still sitting in the same position. Sannakka told him what had happened. Appa sat in front of Amma and said, get up, eat something. She bent and touched his face. Suddenly she started crying. Appa just sat there with his head bent. Then Amma took out her two bangles from her wrists and placed them in front of Appa. He slowly made her get up and led her to the room. Sannakka held me tightly and started crying. For a long time, the bangles were just lying there. Finally, Doddakka closed the front door, made us both get up and took the bangles and went into the room.

Earlier, whenever somebody came home, I was told to sit in the room and they would close the door. The door was not opened until after the guest left. I don't know if Appa knew of this. Now, as soon as the sound of the gate is heard, as soon as it is known that somebody is coming, Amma gives me a glance and I get up and go to the room. If I am already in the room when somebody comes home, Amma or Doddakka check on me and close the door softly. Until the guests go, I sit at the window and look at the road. I do not mind that I am locked in the room. In fact, I also do not want to show my face to anybody.

Appa had taken loans, it was the only time that Appa was in debt. He pawned the gold bangles and chain that was reserved for Doddakka's wedding. Some of Amma's gold also was given away. Sannakka never had any gold. Anyway, Appa pawned all the gold and paid back the loan. He did not take out a loan again. Somehow, we are managing to live in this house. We never felt any shortcomings. Even if we felt anything, it would be forgotten the next day.

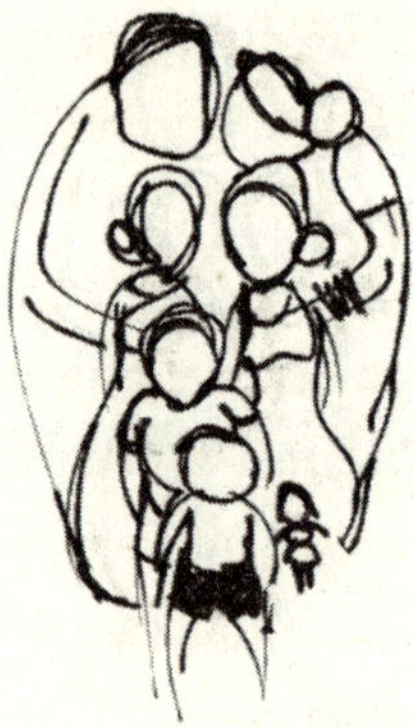

There is a big green book in our house. It has a shining green leather cover. It is full of photos. Some photos are stuck on black paper. It is covered by a thin butter sheet. Then more photos. There are a couple of photos of Appa-Amma's wedding. There is a studio photo of Appa and Amma wearing garlands. Amma looks adorable and slim. Appa is standing upright, as if angry with somebody about something. Next to them is a pot with a big plant. There is another photo with Ajji, Amma's mother. She looks exactly like Amma. She must be shy; she has covered her cheeks with her palms. That is the only photo of Ajji there is. Ajji died when I was two years old, I am told. When I was brought home, Ajji had cried. She predicted that I would bring good luck to the home. She insisted that Appa should go to Kateel Durgaparameshwari to offer prayers. There is another photo. Appa, Amma, Doddakka, Sannakka, Anna (when they were all young). Appa is sitting on a chair. Sannakka is sitting on Appa's lap. Amma is standing behind Appa. Doddakka is standing next to Amma. Between them there is another girl, who looks exactly like Amma. She has her hand over Doddakka. Don't know who she is. Anna is sitting on a mat in front. Some photos have turned yellow. In some other photos lots of people are sitting in a line eating lunch. These are the wedding photos of Appa and Amma. I don't know who those people are. Sometimes when bored Amma picks up this book and tells stories about each photo. In one photo Anna is sitting on a tricycle. There are photos of everyone except mine. On the last two sheets there are some marks. Like something was stuck on and then pulled off. Maybe there was one photo of me, who knows. I have never asked anybody. There is one photo of Amma. Two days before her wedding. She is alone. She is laughing, looking very beautiful. Every time I open this book, I keep looking at this photo. I have never seen Amma laugh like that.

If I sit in a chair in the room and look at the road, our compound gate is not visible. When the sound of the gate being opened is heard, either Amma or Sannakka opens the door. Usually, Doddakka does not come out at all. If there is nobody at home then she opens the door. Come to think of it, who comes to our house? Milkman, vegetable woman who comes on alternate days. My teacher comes daily. Occasionally Anna's friends. They don't come in, but stand outside the gate and call out to him. Coming, Anna shouts and runs out. Earlier, once a month somebody would come with an alliance for Sannakka. It's almost two years now since all that has stopped. I was sitting watching the road. The gate opened. Amma went out shouting, who is it? Maybe she opened the door. All of a sudden, I heard Amma crying loudly. Doddakka and Sannakka also ran out. I heard everybody whispering and sobbing. I couldn't wait any more. I got down from the chair and went and stood at the door and peeped. A woman had come. She looked exactly like Amma. Amma, Doddakka, Sannakka and that woman were hugging each other and sobbing. Finally, Amma led that woman into the house holding her hand. That woman saw me standing behind the curtain and peeping. Her face looked shaken when she saw me. She looked at Amma questioningly. Amma said, wiping her tears, Papoo. She looked at me, smiled and put out her hands as if calling me. I did not stir. Doddakka said, she is calling, come. I emerged slowly out of the curtain and went near her. She knelt down and hugged me tight. She said, I am your eldest sister. I did not believe her. I looked at Amma. Amma nodded indicating, yes. The Hosakka (new elder sister) held my hand and took me inside. Walking in, Amma turned and looked back. Hosakka said, it's okay, he will not come in, he won't mind. I looked back. A man was standing leaning against the compound wall. He had sort of light green eyes. A thin moustache under his nose. He looked like a prince. He had a scar, a dark line, on his forehead on the right side. It actually looked good. He saw me and waved at me. I waved back. All of us walked in. For about half an hour Amma was in high spirits. She made coffee for Hosakka. They all chatted excitedly. Hosakka made me sit on her lap. I said, I am grown up, but she insisted. Somehow, I liked Hosakka. But then, they had said the other elder sister had died, so who was this? I must ask Sannakka.

One night Sannakka came screaming from the room. We were all sitting in the hall. She was holding a sheet of paper. She was cleaning the room and had found this letter, she said. She handed it over to Appa. He read it and placed it in front of Amma. Amma can read but very slowly. She has to go alphabet by alphabet. What can I understand, you read, what is it, she asked. Your son has written it, said Appa, picking it up and reading. The letter said Anna was scared, Appa's generation were lunatics, elder uncle had hanged himself because he was scared of this, the younger uncle is also mad, luckily, he left without troubling anybody, brother (that is I) is also like this from birth, one sister is halfwit, the other has fits, nobody in their right sense can survive in this house, if he continued to live in this house, he would either hang himself or go mad, that is why he was running away from home, forget me and let me make a living somewhere, he had written. This time Amma did not cry. Doddakka started crying; not loudly, but under her breath. She cried the whole night. Nobody knows what Sannakka was feeling. She was never talkative to start with. Amma got up and left. Appa remained sitting in the hall the whole night. I have complete faith in my Tangi. Nothing will happen to her.

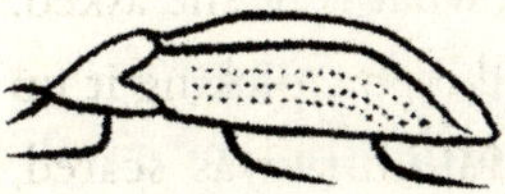

One day I found out how Appa became a debtor. Appa had a friend. Whenever Appa travelled out of station for a few days to purchase clothes, he would ask this friend to take care of the shop. A couple of times he had asked Anna to take care of the shop but he had refused. Appa had no other choice. Since he couldn't shut the shop for so many days, he would ask his friend to take care of it. He would tell Amma that he is a Brahmin and trustworthy. But he fiddled with the accounts and one day when caught, he ran away. When Appa checked the accounts, he found out that the man had raised a loan on the shop account. Appa had to repay that loan.

I fainted just as I was sitting in the chair. I blacked out and fell down. Maybe I shouted while falling because Amma came running. My head was aching. Amma said I had fever. Who should go to the shop to tell Appa? Finally, Sannakka went. Amma cautioned her to go carefully on the road. Tangi is also growing bigger and becoming adamant. Whenever I get a headache, Amma suffers. Tangi also screams for her attention. I resist but still Amma makes me lie down next to her and presses my head. What she can get her hands on she applies to my head. I feel sorry for Amma. Even when Sannakka offers to apply the ointment Amma says no and does not allow her to. Tangi does not go to Sannakka.

Sweeping, sprinkling water and drawing rangoli designs in the front yard every morning is Doddakka's job. At night it is usually very late by the time Amma and Sannakka wash the vessels, do sundry work and go to bed. So it is Doddakka's job to wake up early by 4.30 or 5 in the morning, and take care of the front yard work. That day Amma woke up and came out of the room. She was hit by a cool breeze. The door was open. Amma went out and saw that the front yard was not washed or the rangoli drawn. Amma panicked and rushed to our room. Sannakka and I were still sleeping. Amma woke up Sannakka. I also woke up. Amma asked where Doddakka was. Sannakka sat up quickly saying, don't know. The mat on which Doddakka slept was neatly rolled and kept in the corner. Appa came in asking what all the noise was about so early in the morning. Everybody realised Doddakka was not at home. Nobody knew when or where she went. There was no other man besides Appa in the house to go searching for her. Appa went looking for her and returned in the hot afternoon without any result. That day he didn't open the shop. After lunch he went again searching for her. He returned at night. Where to look for her? Did she have any friends? We didn't know. I don't remember her ever going out alone. She always went out with Amma. Never with Sannakka, because she always fights with her. Appa shut the shop for two more days and searched for her. He posted letters to the village asking if she had gone there. She had not gone there. Then where did she go?

Appa returned early from the shop. Amma gave him coffee. Appa was holding the cup in his palm and was sitting there without drinking. All of a sudden he said, he must have come, I think I saw him in the market. Amma could not make out who. She asked, who? Your son, he walked away as if he didn't see me, said Appa. You should have gone and brought him, said Amma. Who knows if it was him or not, I thought it was him, he rushed on, I had this cloth bundle and couldn't chase him, let him go, never mind, if he does not care for the family, why should we bother, he said, gulping down the coffee at one go.

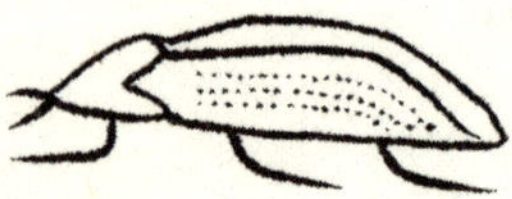

Sometimes I wonder if what Anna said before running away is true. Really, why should all this happen to us?

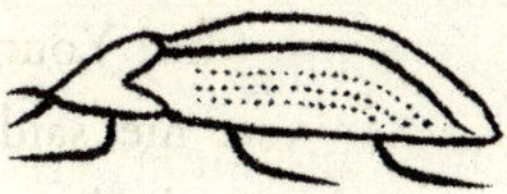

Hosakka apparently had not died. She had eloped with somebody. One day Sannakka told me. Hosakka was going to typing class. Nobody knew the teacher's name, but everybody knew that he was a Muslim. She eloped with him. Nobody at home had any clue about it. Hosakka was moving around with him, after class he was escorting her back home. Rumours started flying. Ours is not a big city. Very soon the rumour reached Appa's ears. That night Appa asked Hosakka and she denied it. Appa kept quiet. For some time nobody spoke of it at home. Hosakka was returning home on time. One day Appa's client told him that he saw Hosakka with a Muslim boy in a park. That night Appa shouted at her. Usually, Appa does not beat girls and so he didn't beat her. That night he made her promise on God that she would cut off this friendship.

After a couple of days, it was in the town's newspaper that such and such girl, daughter of such and such man is moving about with a Muslim boy and is a black spot on the Brahmin community. That paper was run by a Brahmin. That night for the first time Appa beat her. He stopped talking to her. She also did not try to talk to him. Some people from the community came to advise Hosakka. They came in big groups. They also threatened Appa that if he does not control his daughter and if this continues, they would complain to Sringeri Mutt and get the family expelled from the community. From that night stones started being pelted on our home. Somebody would knock on the door at night and run away. They would loudly call out her name and whistle. As days passed more crowds started coming home to give advice. They would just bang on the door and walk in. Appa started fearing any banging of the door. Sometimes he would sit up at night saying, somebody is banging on the door. Finally, one day, Hosakka eloped. She left a letter stating that she had married the boy and they were leaving the town. She did not say where they were going. She had promised in front of God yet ran away so Appa declared that she was dead to the family. He made everybody at home swear that they will not talk about her. Maybe from that day Appa got angry with God. Sannakka narrated the entire incident to me at night, secretly. I felt pity towards Hosakka.

After Doddakka disappeared, Sannakka has become very dull. Earlier we would often sit on the washing slab at night. She would always take me with her. Papanna come, she would call. But now she goes to sit there daily. She does not call me. Of course, she won't object if I go but she doesn't call me like before. I don't want to go there on my own. Once I went. She was just sitting still, staring at the Kakada flower bush. I couldn't make out if she knew I was there. I went silently without making any noise and sat next to her. I looked at her face. She was crying. Her cheeks were wet. After some time, she said Papanna, when am I going to die? That means she knew I was there.

The stranger who had come home had long hair. He was wearing white pants and a white shirt. He had dark goggles on. Maybe the door was open, we didn't know that he had entered the house. He came straight into the hall, sat on the chair and called out Amma's name. I came out of the room to see who was calling Amma. Amma came running from the kitchen. Maybe she was in the middle of work because her hands were wet. Right behind her Sannakka also came running. The stranger who was combing his hair got up on seeing Amma and touched her feet. He placed the small comb in his back pocket and sat down again. Amma looked at me and said, Maama (meaning, her brother). I didn't understand who is this Maama. I just stared at him. He said, kyaabaa, prince. I smiled. Amma said, what's that Muslim language, talk properly. Maama made a sign with his hand, calling me to him. I didn't go. Finally, after Amma forced me, I went to him. He said, have you given birth to a girl, how shy he is, and pulled me next to him. He held my hand and kept tapping it. He had applied some scented oil to his hair. It had a strong smell. Amma sat on the floor before him. Sannakka sat behind her. Amma asked, when did you come? Some four days ago, he said. From where did you come, where were you all these days? I had gone to Baroda and then to Kalkatta, for four years I was doing this and that, got bored, went to Burma, what prince, do you know where is Burma, in India or foreign? I said, next to India. Good, I am coming from Bombay, for some days I will be here, after that god knows where. Did you make any money or what? Yes, I did make, but I also spent it all, now bankrupt. Will you not marry? That is one evil left in my useless life. As he was talking, he kept shaking his leg. He didn't stop patting my hand also. What sort of an elder sister are you, you didn't even offer me coffee even after fifteen minutes of my arrival! Ayyo, I am so forgetful, Amma tapped her forehead and tried to get up. Sannakka didn't let her get up and went to the kitchen. I was standing next to the chair. Maama was talking funny. Sannakka brought coffee. Taking the coffee cup, Maama said, what my niece, will you marry me? Sannakka sat down with a long face. Why make your face long, will I marry you as soon as asked? Sannakka replied equally pointedly, who wants to marry you, no house, no job, I don't have any wish to be a hungry nomad, understand? He laughed loud and said, not bad, your daughter can really talk. He put down the cup and said to spread a mattress, I will sleep till my Bhaava (brother-in-law) comes. Then he went out to the toilet. I don't know where this Maama was all these days, nobody had ever spoken about him in the house. Come to think of it, we don't know many from Amma's family.

Appa never comes home in the afternoon, unless for a reason. That day he came home in the afternoon. When I came to know Appa had come, I came out of the room. Appa sat leaning against the wall in the hall. He was silent. He looked pale. He had a newspaper next to him. Nobody knew yet that he had come home. Amma and Doddakka had not come out of the kitchen. Sannakka must have been in the backyard. Even she did not come in. I went and told Amma that Appa had come. She stopped her work and came out wiping her hands with the edge of her saree. I followed her. She asked Appa if he wanted coffee. Appa did not speak. By then Doddakka came in and stood looking at Appa. Amma asked again if she should prepare coffee. Appa shook his head indicating, no. He thrust the newspaper aside and said, I must go to Calicut immediately. Shocked, Amma sat before him. He stared at her face. Appa's eyes welled up. Amma asked what had happened. Appa said he has gone, the police had come to the shop, I have to go with them. Amma did not understand anything. She kept looking at his face. Then she looked at the newspaper. Anna's photo was printed on it. She understood. By then Sannakka had picked up the newspaper. She cannot read properly. She gave it to me. I saw. Appa got up suddenly and said, pack a couple of clothes in a bag, I will go and see, let that also happen. He went into their room. Amma ran behind him. I clutched the paper and came to our room. For a long time, I kept staring at Anna's photo. Where is Calicut? How far is it from here? He had written he was going to Madras, why did he go to Calicut? I opened the newspaper and read. It was printed in bold letters: J P calls for total revolution. More than 200 college students arrested in Gujarat.

I went to the backyard. It had rained. The moon was partly visible. Several small pools had formed in the yard. Each pool reflected a moon. The backyard was filled with several moons. Just like, when the wind blows, the guava flowers get scattered all over the courtyard, a strong wind had swept and the moon had fallen in bits and pieces in our backyard.

It was in the paper. The police had been searching for Anna for a week. He was escaping them, constantly moving from place to place. That night they raided the hostel and caught him, along with eight or ten other boys. That night in Kerala about 200 boys were arrested, all college students, it seems. When the police caught Anna and his friends, they had some papers, it said. Anna was thrashed mercilessly at the station. He took it all without uttering a word. They thrashed him the entire night. At some point of time, he had died. In the morning at six o'clock the police brought his body and handed it over to his friends. That is what the boys said. He had not eaten properly since a week and was very tired. For two days the police searched for his identity. Finally, they found our house. Even in his end, Anna did not give up his obstinacy.

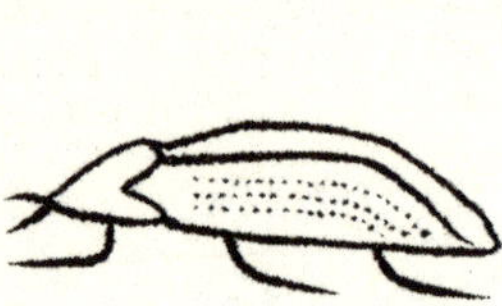

That night I was taken to the Shetty doctor. With every passing day, I was fainting more often. Shetty doctor checked me and spoke to Appa for a long time. Appa returned to where I was sitting. He hugged me tight. Looked like he had cried. He did not talk to me. He just picked me up and walked out. I said I am big now but he did not put me down. He carried me till we reached home. Even at home, he sat next to me and had dinner. Till I fell asleep he was with me. I think he walked out only after I slept. Sometime in the night I woke up and saw Amma sitting near me. She was just staring at me.

Ours is an open house, the door is never shut. Earlier, after Appa left for the shop and Anna went to school, Sannakka would shut the door and latch it. Whenever somebody came, hearing the gate opening or when the visitor called out, Sannakka or if she was busy, Amma, would open the door. It is mostly Sannakka. Sometimes if all of them were busy they would not hear the door being tapped. I would hear it as I would be sitting in the room watching the road. But I was not supposed to open the door. That was Appa's rule. Sannakka had fought with Appa on that. After that it was decided that if somebody comes, I must go in and tell them that somebody has come and return to the room. Till I returned to the room Amma or Doddakka or Sannakka would be calling out, coming. They would open the door only after I went inside the room. During the day whenever we had visitors, I had to go in and inform them and return to the room. This constant opening and closing of the door had become a big issue. Finally, we decided to keep the door unlatched all the time. The people who usually come are the vegetable seller woman, milk vendor, Appa during lunch time, Anna after school and the Kalayi Saaba. Those who were familiar would open the gate and walk straight in. Strangers would stand at the gate and call out to Amma. Eventually we kept the door ajar, without even closing it. On hearing the gate opening, if I was out in the hall, I would run to the room and close the door and would sit and watch the road. One day Appa walked in and said, why can't you close the door. Amma replied, which thief will walk in and even if he comes there is nothing for him to steal. Appa went silent. From that day we stopped closing the door. In the morning the door would be opened to draw rangoli and it would be closed only at night before going to bed.

Every day the teacher comes exactly at 5.30 in the evening. I always know about his arrival. He rings the cycle bell as soon as he reaches and leans the cycle against the wall. Then he walks in. Usually, I sit ready from 5 o'clock. If I am late in coming, he sits, waiting, staring at the roof. Sometimes dozing. On the days I have fever, he comes and takes a look at me and leaves. When he enters the room the first thing he does is to remove the small tin belt he wears around his right ankle, to hold the pyjama in place so it won't get caught in the cycle chain, and puts it carefully in his bag. Then he sits on the mat. He always carries that cloth bag. I don't know what is in it. Sometimes when Appa comes, teacher takes out either *Prajamatha* or *Samyukta Karnataka* and reads something from it to Appa. He always teaches sitting cross-legged, leaning against the wall. Sometimes he leans towards one side and lets out a loud fart. He always farts when my head is bent down as I write. The sound is loud. I don't lift my head up. But he pats my head and says hey, you thief! Sometimes I don't know what happens to him, he lets out a series of farts. After each fart, he sighs loudly. At such times he doesn't say hey, thief!

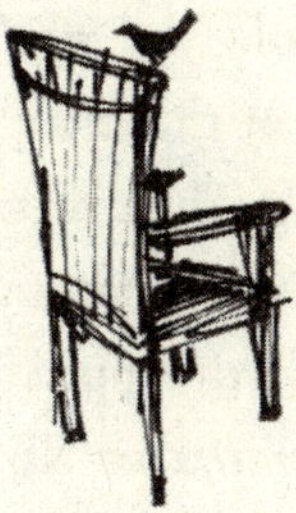

It must be two or three years since Anna died and Doddakka disappeared. Hosakka visits us at least a couple of times in a month. Hosakka always comes when Appa is not at home. Mostly by afternoon. How does she know that Appa is not at home? When Appa goes out of town to purchase clothes she comes early in the morning and stays till evening. How does she know that Appa is not in town? When she comes while Appa is out of town my heart beats fast, I am scared that Appa may come home. Whenever she comes, she brings a drawing book or colour pencil or pen for me. On her previous visits, she brought a story book. Every month she brings children's magazines, *Chandamama* or *Kasturi*. I have to read and hide them before returning them to her. If Appa sees them he will ask who brought them and we cannot say Hosakka. That becomes an issue. So, Sannakka hides them inside her bed roll. Of late, Tangi is growing up. She repeats what I say. She sits up now. If she wants something and does not get it, it is impossible to calm her. Amma keeps saying, from whom did Ammayya get this stubbornness. Everybody calls her Ammayya. If you call her Ammayya she quickly turns towards you.

A sparrow flew into the house. It couldn't find its way out. It kept flying all over the room, chirping. It would sit on the light and then on the photo. I opened the door wide to let it go out. But poor thing, it could not find its way out at all. It couldn't go out through the window either. I took a towel and swung it to make it go out. Poor thing, it must have gotten scared. It started flying about rapidly. I sat down and watched it. Suddenly I felt a sharp pinprick on the back of my head. I turned around and there was nobody. It happened again. This time it was like somebody was pricking me with eight or ten big needles. I heard the sparrow's noise but could no longer see it. Then gradually the sparrow's sound also stopped. I screamed, Amma. Sannakka, I screamed. By the time Amma and Sannakka came running, I had vomited. Green vomit. My head was aching too much. I only know that Amma came and held me.

Sannaka had gone to the Setty's grocery shop to get something. She did not return for quite some time. Amma was pacing in and out of the house. Who should go out to look for her? Only Amma and I were at home. I could not go out during the day. And Amma had not stepped out of the house alone for many years. Amma could not take it anymore; she sat outside the main door and started crying into her pallu. I went and sat next to her. After some time, four-five people came to our house. One elderly man was holding Sannakka's arm and walking with her. Seeing them, Amma stood up and I slid back into the room. A little later I heard the elderly man saying to Amma, don't allow her out alone amma, she has seizure-fits and she fell down on the road, it took some time for her to wake up, she is a grown-up girl and it is not good for her. I heard them going away. I came out. Sitting leaning against the wall, Sannakka was shivering. Her hair was all messed up and dusty. Amma went and clung to her. Sannakka did not talk. She sat there shivering.

After Doddakka disappeared the housework has increased. No, not increased. But Sannakka and Amma have to do her work also. Sannakka is a light sleeper anyway. Now she wakes up by four o'clock and finishes off the front yard work in a jiffy. When Doddakka was drawing the rangoli, it was like a proper drawing. The lines looked straight like they were drawn using a scale. The dots she put before she started drawing would not be seen at all after the rangoli was completed. One day she would draw a flower, the next day some pattern. One day a square design and the next day a circle design. Even visitors did not feel like stepping over it. They would walk around it. For Deepavali, Yugadi festivals she would draw in colour. The entire street would come to see it. The next day early morning she would rub it all out, no matter who requested her not to. Sannakka draws the rangoli as a ritual. Not straight like Doddakka but all crooked. But still like Amma says at least it makes the front yard look good.

At night after everybody went to bed, the long-haired Maama would go to the backyard and sit on the washing slab. After he came, Sannakka and I have stopped going there. I felt like peeing badly. I told Sannakka and she took me to the backyard. The long-haired Maama was sitting there. Come prince, he called. I looked at him and went to the toilet. Sannakka stood there, waiting for me. You go in, I am here, I will bring him, long-haired Maama said. I think she must have gone in because when I came out after peeing the long-haired Maama was sitting alone. After I washed my feet, he called me, come prince. I went to him. He moved a little and said, sit. I sat. He was holding a cigarette in his right hand, smoke coming out of his mouth. You must become a big hero, he said and put his hand on my shoulder. For a long time he was silent. He was smoking. He didn't take his hand off my shoulder. He threw away the butt and sat quiet. Then he asked, prince, shall I tell you a story? I nodded. He lit another cigarette, puffed deeply and after a minute exhaled from his nostril and started telling the story. For some time as he spoke smoke came out of his mouth and nostrils. There was once a prince, some saint, for some silly reason, cursed his parents that your son will be born like a frog, as per the curse the son was born like a frog, the parents fell at the saint's feet and cried, begging to save their son, the saint also pitied them and said when a girl picks him up and kisses him on her own he will become human again, so there was no other go, the parents put him in the pond and waited, some years passed nobody came, one day, maybe it was Yugadi, the new year's feast, people had come from all over to the house, among them was this girl from the desert, she did not know fear, she was playing with others and came to the pond, she did not know that one could have so much water in the house, in her house they had water only in buckets, she put her feet in the pond and sat there, the frog prince was jumping around in the pond, she did not know what a frog was, when there was no water in her place how will she know a frog, she put out her hand in the water and picked up the frog, green frog looked very cute, on an impulse she kissed the frog, in a flash the frog turned into a prince, she married him and they lived happily ever after, how is it? he asked, threw the butt and said, come let us go in and walked in. I followed him.

Sometimes my headache becomes unbearable. I tie a cloth tight around my head and sit. When Amma and Sannakka see me like that they rush to me and hold me. Sannakka calls out to Amma. Amma then comes and makes me lie down with my head on her lap and presses it. Till my headache disappears and I sleep. Sometimes if I say my headache has gone and try to stand up she chides me and insists that I sleep. Of late Ammayya does not like anybody else lying on Amma's lap. Even if Amma says, you sleep on one lap, she does not like it. She wants Amma entirely to herself. She will not go to Sannakka also. Finally, Sannakka takes my head on her lap and keeps pressing it. Sometimes I wonder why this headache bothers me. When I get a headache, Amma cries. I can't take that. Does she know something that I don't know?

We had a small radio at home. Somebody had gifted it to Appa, I am told. Appa leaves early in the morning and returns late at night. Sometimes he comes home for lunch. There are also days when he comes home for coffee in the evening. On days he doesn't come home, I don't know where he has his lunch. When he has to take me to Shetty doctor he comes early in the evening. On such occasions Amma makes a cup of coffee for him. I also get a cup of coffee. Both of us drink coffee and wait for it to get dark before starting out. Appa hardly listens to the radio. The radio can be carried to anywhere in the house. But mostly Sannakka has it. Doddakka is not very fond of songs. Actually she hardly has time for all that. Amma will be desperate to finish the work and sleep at night. Sannakka finishes all her work by evening and takes the radio. She sits either under the guava tree or on the washing slab listening to the radio till it gets dark. That is how she has learnt film songs, *Devaranama* et cetera. She sings along when these songs are played on the radio. Sometimes if I am sitting next to her, she tells me which film that song is from. On Sunday afternoons the soundtrack of a film is broadcast. On such days she sits outside with the radio. She listens to the soundtrack and cries her heart out. One day the radio stopped working. For some days it made weird noises and eventually went totally silent. After that we have not had another radio in this house. Now, any song that is heard in this house is that of Sannakka singing.

Appa took me to Shetty doctor again. We did not walk. He got a tonga. Amma also accompanied us. Amma cautioned Sannakka a hundred times to take care of the house before getting on to the tonga. Sannakka stood at the gate, looking at us till we went out of sight. Shetty doctor comes at a regular time. That day too he was already there. Some people were waiting outside. Appa straightaway took me in. Amma came running behind us. As soon as Shetty doctor saw us he said, let's go and walked out with us. He straightaway went to his car. We all got into his car. We went to a hospital. There was another doctor there. He spoke just like Shetty doctor. He asked very softly, where my head ached, what happens when it aches, do I feel faint and all. I pointed to my head in the front and said, it hurts here. He touched the back of my head and asked, here? I said it pains there too. He didn't say anything but walked out of the room. Shetty doctor also followed him. After some time Shetty doctor came and called me. I went with him. There was a big bed there. Something big was hanging over it. I got scared. Shetty doctor touched me on the shoulder and said, nothing, it's only X-ray. The other doctor made me stand at one place and asked me not to shake my head and went inside. After a minute he came out and called me out. After making me sit with Appa and Amma, both the doctors went in again. We sat there for a long time. Appa was holding my hand, pressing my palm. Amma sat there without speaking, pressing her saree pallu to her mouth. Then Shetty doctor came out and said, come, and dropped us home in his car. Amma and I got out. He asked Appa to stay back in the car. After Amma and I got out they both left in the car.

That day Hosakka had come. It was afternoon. Appa had gone out of station to purchase clothes. When she came I was in the room. All of a sudden everybody was talking loudly. They were laughing also. I went in. All of them were sitting in the hall. Sannakka was sitting next to Hosakka and holding her hand. Amma was sitting in front of Hosakka. There was a box of sugar in front of Amma. Amma called me, Papanna, come, and she took out some sugar from the box and gave it to me. I took it and put it in my mouth. Sannakka pressed Hosakka's hand to her cheek and said, it's three months for Hosakka. I didn't understand. But all of them were laughing. I have rarely seen all of us laughing like this. Amma was telling Hosakka something, you have to do this, you should not do this, eat this, don't eat this, I wish you could deliver here but you know how it is. They all drank coffee and sat chatting. I went into the room. I sat at the window and looked out. He was standing leaning against the compound. The green-eyed man. He was looking at the window. Maybe he sensed I had come into the room. He waved at me. I also waved back. He smiled. He made a sign with his hand asking if I had eaten. I nodded. Again, he made a sign asking if I will not sleep. I shook my head, indicating no. Suddenly he looked aside. He moved away from the compound. He looked scared. After a minute all noise from the hall stopped. I got up and went to the hall. Appa was standing there. He was holding a bundle of clothes in both his hands. Amma was staring at Appa, very scared. Sannakka was sitting behind Hosakka, looking down. Hosakka was looking at Appa and Appa was looking at her. Amma said, she is three months. Hosakka did not speak. She got up and went to Appa and bent down and fell at his feet, touching them. She sat there on her knees. Appa did not speak. He just said, hmm, and went towards the room. Before going inside he stood at the door and said, call him in, why is he standing in the road? Saying this he went inside and closed the door. Hosakka started crying. Why was she crying when Appa did not scold her?

Tangi is now very active. She now stands up, holding onto the wall. She tries to run towards anybody who calls her. After taking two steps from the wall, she falls down. Now Ammayya is not scared of me. She comes to me also when I call. She had a piece of coconut in her mouth and was drooling all over. It would fall from her mouth and she would pick it up and put it back in her mouth. I called out, Ammayya, and went to her. But before I could reach her, I crashed to the ground and fainted.

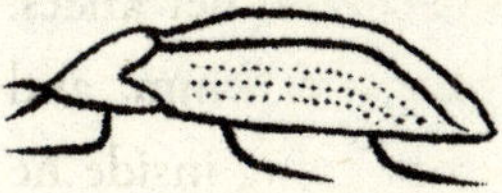

I have been at Shetty doctor's hospital for two days now. Sannakka or Amma or the Maama with long hair stay with me. Mostly the long-haired Maama. When I asked if he was not leaving, he said I will not leave you and go anywhere, prince. Intense headache. I also have seizures. I am fainting five to six times in a day. Appa said I am here because of that. They keep conducting some or the other tests daily. When I look out of the window, it's all blurred. It all looks double. Writing is also a problem. That's why my book was not brought. After I insisted, they gave it to me. Sometimes I can't see what I have written.

I know I will not survive. Nobody needs to tell me that. I am fed up with this headache. I told Appa I wanted to go home. He asked the doctor. The doctor must have agreed, the same evening Appa hired a tonga and brought me home.

From the window I put out a fistful of rice. The tree is full of birds but not a single bird comes to eat from my palm. I am waiting. Maybe tomorrow or the day after they may come. Daily I put out my hand and wait. Sometimes though the tree is full of birds I cannot see even a single bird. Sometimes I can't see the tree. I can only hear the bird noise.

Amma came in carrying Tangi on her hip. I was sitting facing the window and writing. I turned. Amma was holding something. I couldn't see. Tangi is blurred. Again road....

My name is Uma Rani. Everybody calls me Ammayya. After I got married, I came to Hosadurga with my husband. My husband is a tehsildar. So, we have to keep changing towns every now and then. Now we are in Belgaum. I have three children. After Appa passed away Amma stayed with us. She passed away some five months ago. The other day I was cleaning Amma's trunk and found this notebook. I don't know who has written this. I believe I had an elder brother. If I really try hard, I can vaguely remember his face. His photo is not available. He must have written this book. I have an elder sister. Quite aged. She is in the mental asylum in Bangalore. We go visit her sometimes. Now we have to go to Athani for a program. The car is waiting...

ALSO IN TIGERBACKS IN SPEAKING TIGER

THE DREAM NARRATIVE

The Dreams of God and Mortals in Classical Hinduism

Wendy Doniger

Dreams. Illusions. Reincarnation. Karma. Dreams are a serious matter in Indian myth and religions, especially Hinduism. But are they *maya* (illusion), *lila* (God's play), or an awakening to our real selves? Are we living in a dream dreamt by the Author of the universe as we know it? Are dreams, then, an insight into the reality of that universe? Do they prove the 'nothingness' of the world we see or the substantial reality of 'illusion' itself?

Wendy Doniger is the author of several acclaimed and bestselling works, among them, *Winged Stallions and Wicked Mares: Horses in Indian Myth and History*; *The Hindus: An Alternative History*; *The Ring of Truth: Myths of Sex and Jewelry*; *Dreams, Illusion and Other Realities*; and translations of the *Rig Veda* and the *Kamasutra* (with Sudhir Kakar). She is the Mircea Eliade Distinguished Service Professor of the History of Religions at the University of Chicago. She has also taught at the School of Oriental and African Studies, University of London, and the University of California, Berkeley.

CATEGORY: Non-fiction | PRICE: ₹499 | ISBN: 978-93-5447-215-2

ALSO IN TIGERBACKS IN SPEAKING TIGER

THE LAW OF DESIRE

Rulings on Sex and Sexuality in India

Madhavi Menon

Though India's laws and courts claim to know what they mean when they declare an expression of desire immoral or criminal, obscene or unnatural, upon inquiry, they turn out to be building on very weak and often casteist and patriarchal assumptions. Thus we have the law struggling to 'rescue' 'fallen women', for sex work cannot be work, but a sign of immorality; a Supreme Court judge can exonerate the artist M.F. Husain on charges of obscenity, but also claim that 'obscenity lies in the eyes of the beholder', leaving us wondering how, then, the law can ever define what's obscene; and while a court may declare that the 'third gender' has fundamental rights, no one really knows what fundamental rights have to do with gender in the first place.

Madhavi Menon is professor of English at Ashoka University, and writes on desire and queer theory. She is the author of *Infinite Variety: A History of Desire in India*; *Wanton Words: Rhetoric and Sexuality in English Renaissance Drama*; and *Indifference to Difference: On Queer Universalism*. She is also the editor of *Shakesqueer: A Queer Companion to the Complete Works of Shakespeare.*

CATEGORY: Non-fiction | PRICE: ₹499 | ISBN: 978-93-5447-115-5

GOING

Stories of Kinship

Keki N. Daruwalla

A man drifts away from family and home and becomes a monk, yet nothing fills the void. The only constant are dreams and hallucinations where his mother sometimes appears. Another son retreats to his room, then disappears. It has been ten years and the father, Sudhakar, doesn't want to harbour false hope, but the mother, Hemlata, clings to it. Ardeshir and Firoza face a similar predicament. Only their daughter, Arnavaz, hasn't gone missing; she lives with them, even in her absence. A woman, half-estranged from her mother, comes to visit her grandmother, perhaps for the last time.

Keki N. Daruwalla is one of India's foremost poets and writers. His ten volumes of poetry include *Under Orion*, *The Keeper of the Dead* (winner of the Sahitya Akademi Award, 1984), *Landscapes* (winner of the Commonwealth Poetry Award, Asia, 1987), *Night River* and *The Map-maker*. His first novel, *For Pepper and Christ*, was shortlisted for the Commonwealth Fiction Prize in 2010. He was awarded the Padma Shri in 2014. Most recently, he was honoured with the Poet Laureate award at the Tata Literature Live! Mumbai Litfest, 2017. His work has been translated into Spanish, Swedish, Magyar, German and Russian.

CATEGORY: Fiction | PRICE: ₹499 | ISBN: 978-93-5447-295-4